WILDER

WILDER

Claire Wahmanholm

Lindquist & Vennum Prize for Poetry

Selected by Rick Barot

MILKWEED EDITIONS

Published 2018 by Milkweed Editions
Printed in Canada
Cover design by Mary Austin Speaker
Cover photo by NASA/Goddard/Lunar Reconnaissance Orbiter
Author photo by Daniel Lupton
18 19 20 21 22   5 4 3 2 1
First Edition

Milkweed Editions, an independent nonprofit publisher, gratefully acknowledges sustaining support from the Jerome Foundation; the Lindquist & Vennum Foundation; the McKnight Foundation; the National Endowment for the Arts; the Target Foundation; and other generous contributions from foundations, corporations, and individuals. Also, this activity is made possible by the voters of Minnesota through a Minnesota State Arts Board Operating Support grant, thanks to a legislative appropriation from the arts and cultural heritage fund, and a grant from Wells Fargo. For a full listing of Milkweed Editions supporters, please visit milkweed.org.

Library of Congress Cataloging-in-Publication Data

Names: Wahmanholm, Claire, author.
Title: Wilder : poems / Claire Wahmanholm.
Description: First edition. | Minneapolis, Minnesota : Milkweed Editions, 2018.
Identifiers: LCCN 2018027567 (print) | LCCN 2018028516 (ebook) | ISBN 9781571319951 (ebook) | ISBN 9781571315069 (pbk. : alk. paper)
Classification: LCC PS3623.A35648 (ebook) | LCC PS3623.A35648 A6 2018 (print)
| DDC 811/.6--dc23
LC record available at https://lccn.loc.gov/2018027567

Milkweed Editions is committed to ecological stewardship. We strive to align our book production practices with this principle, and to reduce the impact of our operations in the environment. We are a member of the Green Press Initiative, a nonprofit coalition of publishers, manufacturers, and authors working to protect the world's endangered forests and conserve natural resources. *Wilder* was printed on acid-free 100% postconsumer-waste paper by Friesens Corporation.

CONTENTS

wilder, v.
arch.

1. a. *trans.* To cause to lose one's way, as in a wild
or unknown place; to lead or drive astray; *refl.* to
lose one's way, go astray.
3. *trans.* and *intr.* To render, or become, wild or
uncivilized. *Obs. rare.*

WILDER

DESCENT

Lost in a haunted wood,
Children afraid of the night
Who have never been happy or good
W.H. AUDEN

whose eyes have never really opened;

who were born with bitter seeds sewn
　　beneath our eyelids;

whose eye bulbs glow red when salted;

whose sockets grow tall bitter stalks
　　that sprout small bitter buds
　　that crawl with aphids;

whose faces are wild fields, and fruitless;

whose throats are peeled peaches, and voiceless;

who collect eyeballs like marbles
　　and shoot them around a dirt circle;

who drag sickles across each other's skulls
　　and leave wet symbols

we copy onto paper—tales of ancient children

who vanished in a flood,

who stumbled from the spring,

who hid inside a haunted wood
        to save themselves from drowning.

The ocean calls.

we

cross

six trillion miles of

everlasting night

we

are precious

tendrils of light.

We

may be a sun to someone.

Why should we

be

utterly lost

ADVENT

In the first month of the year
        birds curdled the air.

From our windows we watched them
        clench and billow, their wings beating
        so low to the ground that seeds rose
        from their furrows.

When our ears began to ache from the pressure,
        we sent out our augurs.

A great fire, they said,
        is blowing from the east.

This explained the fevers, the mercury
        that broke the levees of our mouths,
        the apples that dimpled and rotted
        in our orchards, dropping through the leaves
        like heart-sized hailstones.

Behind our windows, we waited for the fire to turn
        even as we watched the horizon
        go red from edge to edge.

Every morning new packs of animals fled
        through our orchards. Every morning
        new apples dropped into the hollows
        of their tracks.

We watched our windows warp and crack,
        thought of our daughters' hot foreheads,

of the fevers we knew would climb and climb
without breaking.

We were out of songs to hum. Our throats were boxes
of soot. In our orchards, no more insect thrum,
no swallow quaver.

How did we dare have children we couldn't save?

If we closed our eyes, the falling apples
sounded like heavy rain.

AFTERIMAGE

After the explosion: the longest night.

The shock spins a dream around us which,
for our protection, refuses to end.

Outside the dream, songbirds fall from the trees
and sing their way to ash.

Inside the dream, we look out the window
at the sun that is not really a sun, which brightens
and brightens until our eyes are melted glass.

We watch our bodies flicker like lightning
against the wall. We watch them fall

and get back up again and fall
and stay down.

With every breath the dream thins like the skin
of a balloon until we can see the inside
and the outside of the dream at the same time,

the birds swooping from the trees to land
beside their own bones,

our bodies reaching down to grab our shadows
by the hands.

AFTERSKY

The blue noonday sky, cloudless, has lost its old look of immensity
LEWIS THOMAS

Note: there has been some speculation about the state of the sky—
    whether it is an infinite mouth dragging its gasp across us
    or whether it is a tent
    or whether it is there at all.

When it is a mouth, we shoot its white teeth down.

When it is a tent, we slit its skin to let in the rain.

When it is not there at all, we rank the shades of nothing according
    to their hue:
        alice blue
        iris blue
        a blue of such majesty it can't be looked at
        pale blue
        a vast and uniform heaven
        ultramarine
        falling through the ocean
        falling asleep
        this eve of blackness
        neat, delicate, deep black
        the black dilated iris
        panic
        the long black trail
        absolutely black and appalling

When the sky is not there at all, we pound stakes through our shoes
    to keep us close to the ground.

We tarp our windows so we are not tempted
        to smash the glass and let the aftersky suck us outward
        like marrow from the bones of our houses.

Black at noon, black in the afternoon.

Black hail falls from somewhere and melts invisibly in the yard.

The grass fattens with alien dew.

the   dark

                              is everywhere
                    is

                    '

a confusion   . We

                                                            are

profoundly

lonely   a   reed

In the

Sea

THE MEADOW, THE RIVER

The meadow unfolded before me,
>	a soft, uncrossable rot.

I tore myself in two along my spine and sent half of me
>	into the night to see if I would make it through.

I waited at the meadow's black mouth.
What news? I practiced asking the grass,
>	the shadows of black-eyed Susans, my boots.

The gone edge of me felt clean against the wind's hand.
The gone edge of me felt bright and hot.

It was hard to see in the dark with just one eye
>	but I thought I could see the other half of me
>	moving slowly across the meadow.

Was I waving, or was that just the wind in my hair?
Was I calling, or did the wind just bend itself across my ear?

I put my foot down and felt the grass rise around it
>	like a river. Like the way a lover might rise
>	from the cold bed of one and pull you under.

I couldn't see anything across the meadow.
I couldn't blink the blackness from my eyes.

In fact there was no meadow.
In fact the river had washed away the grass, the black-eyed Susans,
>	my leg below the knee.

I had sent half of me into that water, and now the gone edge
    fevered for its brother.

My leg untethered itself, then my shoulder, my lung.
Was it wind or water that rushed over my tongue?

we

had

a taste for
error

and

frail   boats

o   ye

16

brave   sailors   in

                                              an

          unexplored

sky.

                              we

          strayed from home

and

failed utterly

on

the shores of space

THE MEADOW, THE LAKE

The meadow is a lake.
The lake is 400 degrees.
The meadow smells like steam,
tastes like heat, feels like ash beneath our feet.
Its wind rings a brass bell in our ears.

On Mars are meadows of magnesium soil
that slope slowly upward until they reach the highest point
in the solar system.

This meadow is not a lake, but an ocean.
Birds fly across it for so long they fall
like ripe fruit onto its face.

Their smallness puts large holes in
the sails of our breath,
which are usually full of billow:
the dutiful bellows of our staying above water.

A pair of swallows pivots out of the steam
on scissor wings. Cut from what ark?

We carve sailcloth shadows out of ourselves
and send them forth into the steam.

We name them after what we have failed to be:
Beautiful-and-Rare; Born-Ultimately-of-the-Stars;
Rippling-with-Life; Bright-Point-of-Light.

They will land on the far side of the meadow
sometime next year, but we will not be there.

We will not watch their rough feet stumble
on the bright grass nor hear them bless
the ground in the thin language of their thin throats.

Steam closes its mouth around the last toe of them.

The meadow is as large as Mars and its miles
are no less red.

                    an

                                        alien

          general
                                   collected

               us

               in

  a dank and forgotten   library
               consecrated to   mold

                              The scholars of the library
 studied

                                        and

mapped

us

;

robots

compiled

the

dead   .

in

large

dissecting

rooms   ,

we
        were

                disintegrated,

        pathetic scattered fragments.
                                        on the library shelves
a book

                                the tragedy of

                our

                                wonder   was in it

WHERE I WENT AFTERWARD

On Earth I had been held,
honeysuckled
           not just by honeysuckle
but by everything—marigolds,
bog after bog of small sundews,
the cold smell of spruce.

This planet is nothing like that.
Here, I comb lank alien grass out of my hair.
I wade through monochrome swarms
of weeds and ankle-high piles of ash.

I used to miss desire, but that was eons ago.
I used to miss the sound of my voice,
but that was before I pulled my name
from my throat like a pit and set fire
to the field of my face. If I stumbled
upon this place again, I would not know it.

When I say my skin is lace, I mean
I used to find it lovely. Now there is nothing
I miss. I hold myself in my arms.
I bend against myself like grass, like this.

BREACH

I found my legs
under the porch

under a woolly layer
of pollen under

a heart-shaped layer
of linden leaves

beneath which my legs
lay with their veins out

with their bones
out with their outer

skin peeled back
like bark from a

lightning-struck
tree.
      Inside them

were colonies
of tiny bright bees.

When I reached to touch
them they swarmed

my eyes which were
already honeyed shut

over two cells
of empty space.

I stood in the dark
and felt their bodies'

soft bullets on what
used to be my face.

   in

         a flash of light,

                                                    I

    made myself

                          a

                                    road

                          ,

                                         an
  Earth,

                               in

         slow

         atoms

                    ,   no

         limit

                                    ,

no

future

HOW I DREAMED THERE

No dreams. I am always awake.

This has made time strange.
I cannot name the number of breaths
I have taken here. Whether they could fill
a single balloon or many millions.

The thought of the balloons
and my lungs filling them
is not a thought but a hallucination.
Like one you would get
from breathing in a mild poison
or standing for too long under the sun.

There have been other hallucinations:
dark birds darting into caves
that disappear when I face them;
a human shape waiting for me
in the middle of a road
I am not on; a herd of dreams
calling my name across the gray desert,
my ears soft in their mouths,
their mouths wide as balloons.

Somewhere on this planet is the machine
that moves them. On the horizon, I see them
rising and setting like moons.

the world is very

distant   . We

know   the

                                        humdrum

                                immensity of space

        . We   know that our universe

                        is

        merely a

glimpse

of   the

end

RED ROVER

We are placed in a field.

We are told to wield our bodies
$\qquad$ against each other

like wrecking balls or rockets,
$\qquad$ to target the weakest links

in the chain
$\qquad$ of other children's bodies—

the surfaces of skin
$\qquad$ that sweat and twitch

without our willing it,
$\qquad$ the millimeters of air

between the palms
$\qquad$ that cannot be gripped

into disappearance—
$\qquad$ and shoot them down.

Rove:
$\qquad$ *to show signs of madness, to shoot randomly,*

to wander,
$\qquad$ *to run someone through with a weapon.*

We pool our redness
$\qquad$ like wealth until the final soldier

is caught in the net of our hands,
                                    a limp bird.

Red rover, red rover,
                        there are worlds

whose waves do not break
                            against the bodies of children.

There are worlds
                of wide, stagnant waters.

Red rover, red rover,
                            send the boats of our bodies

to float in those fields forever.
                                    Send wings for our arms

unspooling between each other
                                like barricade tape,

gauze for the crime scenes
                            of our shadows.

If we are unmendable,
                        weigh our brokenness

with long sleep.
                Cast a spell over us

like a sharp sheet.
                    As ghosts, we float through each other

like soft sheep, bleating.

B

B is for Brown Bear, for berries and beehives, buds and blossoms, a babbling brook. Brown Bear lumbering through the balsam firs toward the baton and bludgeon. See Brown Bear bedeviled as it basks on a sunny boulder, baited as it browses for clover. B is for barbed wire, for how Brown Bear can't bathe in the water because of beasts beneath the waves. Blinded by the baleful white bark of birches, by the bald face of the blank moon, Brown Bear doesn't hear the branch buckle and break. B is for bearing witness. See Brown Bear beclouded, bestarred, benighted by hunters even in the boundless sky. See the polar bear's blanket of blubber, its blithe beatitude. B is for *bang bang*; for ballistics and barricades; for backbones breaking; for breathing or not. B for the blood and badge and bullet. B as in *behave, beware*. As in bereft. B is for baby and for the way some baby bears grow up into big bears and some never do. B is for barren and the burning den. For how bulletins are bursting with the bodies of brown bears and the alphabet is just beginning.

men   wander

            among

                    us   ,
                fierce

                       ,
                       a great

many   .

                We are surrounded

by

Ten thousand
large

animals

who

hunt in packs

. Our
generations

become
extinct

SIMON SAYS

Follow my voice.
Says the space between it and my ear
is a years-long tunnel to creep
on my belly through. So I do.
So I am a worm, a snake, finely made
and inlaid with precious mud.
I am a dog that knows where
the food comes from.
                    Simon says
follow the leader. A ladder appears
and I climb it. A lake appears
and I dive inside it and sink. I drink
my way out and flop on the shore,
a fat fish. Simon says *pick up your fins
and start walking* so I do. I split
my tail in two.
                    Simon says *now run*
and I do. Says *now I have a gun* and *stop
or I'll shoot.* But Simon didn't say,
so I keep running. There are rules
and I know them. There are games
and we animals know how they are played.
If we make it to the woods we are safe.
Each day we run a little farther away.

G

G is for girl, for gosling, silly goose. See her gambol, guileless, from her gabled house. G is for gamble and gambit and game, for the way the girl's galoshes are gilded with grime before she even reaches the gate. G could be any girl, but say it is Gretel. See Gretel glow like a goldfinch in the gloom. See Gretel out in the green gale, gathering graupel the size of grapes in her gorse-torn gabardine. G is for the glade gobbling her up, for *going, going, gone.* If G is for the galloping gelding, it is also for the glue. G is for gag, for Gretel gnawing through the grove's gristle until it gapes and lets her go. G is for Gordian knots of golden hair, for the gap-toothed grimace. See Gretel's gown glazed with glycerin, the gingerbread packed like grout beneath her nails. G is for grit and gritted teeth, for eyes glinting like gallium, for gravid with grief. G is for gene, for Gretel begetting a generation of girls who grow downward into the ground. G is the groundwater and the guts, the groan growing inside of us.

We grow up

frozen

like
icy moons

.

our brothers and sisters
Are

giant snow-balls

.
Every now and then

the ice is vaporized

by

an inferno of

light

THE WITCH

A rich talker, thought the children
from their bone cages. They had been watching
the witch for several days and didn't believe
a word she said. No one ate children anymore.
Not here, at least. And anyway,
not good children. They had already explained this
to the witch so now they said it aloud to each other.

If she were really going to eat us, one said,
she would have done it by now.
And if she were really going to eat us,
said the other, *where's the oven?*
They had heard this was how
it was done, back when it used to be done,
which was a very very long time ago,
if it had ever even happened at all.

The children thought back to the footprints
they had made in the mud of the riverbank.
It had not rained in several days. Someone would see
the footprints and follow them along the river
and find the hut and the children inside it.
Not that there was any danger.

The hut was getting warm. The children
couldn't recognize each other without their
outer layers—their winter coats, their shirts,
their skin. The river flashed through
the woods like an enormous needle,
stitching its dark mouth shut.

D

D is for dragon and damsel, diamond and diadem. For deciduous woods, their dropping leaves. For dew and the dewclaws of deer. For deciduous teeth, delicate as dimes or decimals. For daughters and daughter cells. For Daedalus, who (though dexterous, deliberate, dagger-eyed) could not dam his son's daring. For the dazzling daydream of sun on deep water. For how dizzy the drop. For daughter. D is for danger in daylight or damson dusk. D for the deportation of other people's daughters under drape of darkness. For Daphne and her despair. For becoming forest and for deforestation. For dales and dells full of delphiniums, for their deflowering. For disenchantment. For how daughters disappear and some are found and some are not. For desert, ditch, and dirt; for dogs and dental records. D is for detonation, damage, decibel. For Demeter and desolation and the way December daubs its dullness on the wall. For the way death comes to some doors dressed as a long-gone daughter. D for the dress you press yourself against.

POEM AFTER ALL THE CHILDREN HAVE DISAPPEARED

The body gets used to it, like it gets used to anything. Like walking slowly into a freezing lake. If you can bear the first step you can bear the rest. Soon you've always been neck deep in this lake, your arms have always been oblongs of ice, you've always had trouble staying awake. For a long time I could make myself sad by remembering the faces of specific children I used to know. I swam in this sadness because I liked the way it burned. I let it rise to my ears. I let it soak the corners of my mouth until my mouth became a fat sponge. Now I can't even make my face look surprised. I can't make my face do anything. No one will even make eye contact with a school, most of which have become open-air museums. Rain softens the places where the children sat or stood or hid. The placards are etched with letters and dates that we sweep with our fingers as if we're brushing away flies, or the hair from someone's eyes. We rub the stones with crayon. We are forbidden from removing any bones. I stand before the mossy jungle gym and practice my surprised face. I stand near the water and practice gasping. I put my hand to my mouth and wonder why the woman in the lake is yawning.

AFTERBODIES

Note: there has been some speculation about the state of our bodies—
  whether they survived the blast or are ghosts, etc.

We are so glum we can only drag ourselves in circles
  around the kid-less playgrounds while we wait for an answer.

From the dusty woodchips I pull a warm baby tooth and hold it
  against the red sky. It quivers.

Beneath the jungle gym we find a coloring book of blank bodies
  for us to fill in.

The throat is a burning tire, we sing. *Color it red.*
The chest is a burning homestead, we sing. *Color it red.*
The eyes, the eyes, the head of hair. Red.

We like these paper afterbodies and how we can shut them away
  when we're done. We like the singing.

We want to turn what's left of our skins inside out
  and beat them like rugs, but we can't find the zippers.

Instead, we make up a song whose only words are *Say when*,
  but when the time comes, our tongues can't remember

how to say them. We punch each other red, then blue,
  then black, then into thin white flags.

The wind reminds our bodies how to beg.

W

W is for the war that washes us weary and wordless, that wipes the woods of its whip-poor-wills, waxbills, and wrens. We wade in the deep weeds, whip-wild and writhen by the wind. The woad wilts. War warms the water, weeps onto the leaves of walnut trees and withers them. The willow draws widowhood up from the river. We draw war-wasps, sketch the webbing of their wings as they beat, wondrous. Who would have thought we could be wrist-deep in soil and wring only worms from it. Who could have seen the wreath of weevils break and widen into a welt. Our windmills whirl weakly through the air. W is for the west, for the setting sun wet as a wound. The wheat white with worry. W is a wolf that walks through the wildflowers, its whetted mouth wide. The sort of wolf that would swallow a warren whole. Here comes the winter, weasel-eyed. We pull whorls of red wool from the wire of our fences. In the war-sky, the war-moon waxes and waxes, watchful as a warden or a weapon.

STATE OF EMERGENCY

Of the moon and its red bulb.
Its red bell. Its fleshy alarm that beats

in your ears like the pulse
of a body suddenly surfacing

out of the sky—no—
out of the water, which is facing

the sky. No—it is falling
from the sky and entering the water.

Every body of water is a soft platter.
Every body is soft matter that becomes

even softer when it lands.
Beneath a red moon every surface

sprouts a chalk outline, every
chalk outline breaks into a flock

of birds that rises above the hot
asphalt like steam. Impossible

to breathe in it. Impossible to look
at a surface and not see a body

falling out of the future and softening
itself upon it. State of suspense.

State of holding your breath until
your vision blackens and bends.

at the end   , we   turn
blue   beyond
        imagining .

                              we are in   pain   no

                soft meadows

                        here
              , but our search for them

              is

        long

,

longest

                                                                    at the
.
bottom of a deep well.

we

cast no shadow

BEGINNING

A pulling began from nowhere. Book bindings came unglued, hairline cracks cobwebbed the backs of our hands. Caught in this force we could not call by name, we waited. Down by the river, no more boats. Even the docks had been uprooted and stacked on the shore. For a long time we tried not to move, tried to feel in the air where the pulling was coming from. Groups of us stood with our index fingers licked and raised. How long did we stand before we put our hands to our chests? Irregular thumps. Just there, just here. Kaleidoscope of wrong rhythms. Looking at the night sky, we could see new patches of darkness coming alive. Mornings were suddenly birdless, cloudless, without wind, bright deserts. Now we began to wonder whether we had done wrong things. Or rather, which of our wrong things had been wrong enough. Putting our hands out in the dark of our basements, we felt gaps in the limestone where there had been none. Quarries filled overnight with unidentifiable slurry. Rotten fish slapped their rotten smell on the riverbank. Something was going to happen, had already begun happening, and no one wanted to be here when it finished. There was one way out of the city. Under the streets, a set of sewers led to the sea. Very carefully, we lowered ourselves into their metal mouths, leaving all the lights on in our houses. Whatever was watching us might be fooled. Xenon lamps shone like suns from the sewer walls, burning our skin. Yarn unspooled behind us as we walked deeper and deeper in. Zero—as in *ground*, as in *vanishing point*, as in *where the reckoning begins*.

THE JELLYFISH

We emerged like cicadas from under the catastrophe. We stood on the beach and watched meteoroids plink into the sea. The purple sky was clear. All the jellyfish had washed ashore and sat in thick pulp circles. Their indigo bells bent the sand beneath them at an angle. Somebody prodded one with a stick. The purple sky was clear. We could see inside the jellyfish body: the brick dust and the oil and the teeth lodged in the mesoglea alongside the gonads and the gut and the mouth. We could see the poison pulsing through its glass noodle tentacles. We gingerly bagged the jellyfish as evidence. We too felt like windows. When the sky shone through us, the other side trembled.

Plate tectonics accelerated. The land unstitched itself faster than a prairie fire and left deep lakes in its wake, acres on acres of water pasture. The largest breach was called the Misery Rift. Families were riven down the middle by it. We watched our loved ones' faces fade like rain on soil, thought that if we stood perfectly still for some time, we would someday feel their warm backs meet ours in a new Pangaea of skin. So we stood, our raised arms hardening into stone, our handkerchiefs shredding in the wind. Crows harvested beard lichen from our mouths and replaced it with their husky calls. Songbirds laid eggs in the dips of our clavicles and in the pits of our upturned hands. We had thought the earth was finite, that it was only a matter of time before everything returned to its origin. But the lost ones never reappeared at our backs. We couldn't stand forever. Land was ebbing faster than anyone thought it would. Every morning there was a new, farther stretch of blue.

STILL THE SEA

The rifts in us grew and grew. We couldn't stand the way our hearts staggered through this new vastness, tumbling east and west as though through ocean currents, forgetting where the past was. We started eating soil to anchor them in our chests. We swallowed pebbles. Our hearts did not settle but thumped more wildly, sought sharper stones to bruise themselves on. We forced down slabs of mud, built barricades, but our agony swelled in larger and larger waves. We finally thought to pack our grief in salt, to pull the seawater out of it. Instead, we bittered, undiluted. Our grief beat faster and faster until it broke the walls of its house.

NO STARS

We walked inland. We entered a ruined schoolhouse and stood before the blackboard's blank sea. No waves. No white. We wanted to make a timeline but had forgotten the beginning. I looked out the empty window at the purple light. No stars. When had that happened? And where was the light coming from? I drew a year that was a white boat on a green sea. I whitened the water with waving arms, then smudged them out. We would drown out here. I could already feel the weight of less and less air. I pressed my palm to the board and felt it shudder. We all pressed our palms to the board and left black five-pointed stars that cast no light. Outside, the year went by. Our stars turned beneath the purple sky.

THE PIT

We almost fell into it. We were walking with our noses so low to the ground that we didn't notice the ground was ending. But suddenly darkness. Suddenly space and near weightlessness. We dug in our heels and sat back before it, looked down into its planet-sized mouth. We shaped our mouths to the shape of the pit-mouth, yawned so wide we thought we would split. We built huts next to it, daubed their walls with our muddy handprints. We lit fires and killed wild animals and carved their bones into cudgels, sharpened our eyes until they could wound. From raptors we pulled feathers the length of our arms. When bored, we played augur with our piles of bones, gripped our own thumbs like lucky rabbits' feet, like tiny warm grenades. At night we stood on the cliffs and looked as deep as we could into the eye of the pit. Sometimes we thought we saw a pupil of light. What was so bright that it shone up to us at this height? At night we lay with our eyes glazed but open, squeezing our rabbits' feet until they turned white.

RELAXATION TAPE

We listened to relaxation tapes to help us sleep. The purple sky was too bright and our pillows were made of rawhide, so night after night we lay on our cots while a woman's voice cooed at us over the loudspeakers. We found a comfortable position. We let our legs, then arms, then necks go limp. We knew the script by heart. We would walk down a forest path dappled with light. The sun would feel just right on our faces. The air would be cool but comfortable. We would not panic. *Clench your fists*, said the voice. I clenched my fists. *Focus on where it hurts*. I did. Then I relaxed and let the tension float away like smoke on the wind. Beneath my feet was moss. Beneath my palms, bark. *Remember that you can return to this place whenever you'd like*. We remembered. We felt very comfortable and at ease. We were climbing a gentle hill made of tires. The ground was dappled with bleach. We felt a light breeze. *A scenic lookout awaits you at the top of the hill*. Our bodies were becoming very warm and very heavy. We felt very comfortable and at ease. Bodies were dropping from the trees. *Continue to enjoy this peaceful place. Continue to breathe*.

THE FACTORY

Grubby violet dusk. Everywhere, the tongue-tang of rust. Everywhere, endless grass. We pushed the truck until it stopped beside a huge rhizome of brick and broken glass. We pulled our faces out of its violet shards and stared into the mass of the factory's throat. In buildings like this, some of us had bottled glue, stitched animal-skin coats. We remembered sweet blood in the hinges of our hands, fur in our lungs. Now we clambered over toothless windowsills to land in the factory's hard concrete mouth. Rooms of animal suits, rooms of hooves, of hoses. Dark drains. One by one the others put on their palomino coats. Then were gone, their long legs wounding my throat. Outside, the prairie was empty and hot. Beneath my palm its heaving slowed to a trot, to a walk. Beneath my palm the prairie rolled over and stopped.

RELAXATION TAPE

Nightmares were spreading like oil on water, but there was a tape for that too. As we lay on our rawhide cots, the woman's voice told us to *imagine a scary situation you can't escape from.* We imagined quicksand. We imagined being handcuffed and pushed out of an airplane. We imagined being blinded and locked in a burning house. *Now imagine,* sang the loudspeaker, *that you have grown a pair of wings.* We imagined. *You are flying away from your nightmares, away from the danger.* We flew. We looked down on our fear. *It feels wonderful to fly,* soothed the voice. We closed our eyes and saw a man soaring ahead of us in the sky. His wings were crimson curtains on his back. His wings were skin that flaked and feathered as he flew away from his burning house. We caught the ash on our tongues, but we were *completely safe now*; nothing could reach us up here. We breathed in lungfuls of cloud whose droplets felt nothing like sand grains in our mouths. The airplanes from which we fell were nothing but our own bird-shapes hurtling over the ground.

ALMANAC

We had grown leaky. Our heads were full of fissures that wouldn't seal no matter how tightly we clamped the vises' jaws around our temples. Our scalps wept until only the present rattled in our ears, bone-dry and rabid. We walked around the corner or had been walking for years. We entered the same empty house at the end of the same dirt road. In every room I found a yellow almanac under the bed and read the same page, which told me the time Neptune would rise, the time civil dusk would descend. I pressed the almanac to my head. What was *time*? What was *descend*? Whenever I left the house I would take the almanac with me. I put it under my rawhide pillow, hoping that while I slept, my head would somehow mend. Every night I dreamed of frost spreading across a ragged field, knitting the furrows with its uniform white.

FUSE

One morning we woke with bombs in our bellies. We passed our fingers over the raised, tender red of the sutures. Felt how they made mountain chains and riverbeds. We knew there were bombs beneath them because of the ticking. Like a pulse, but not in line with our pulses. Like an enormous cricket we could tell wasn't alive. Our bellies stayed cold and heavy. When we walked, our feet sank deep in the mud. When we tried to climb trees, the branches broke with a crack, with a tick. No one knew where the bombs had come from. No one knew how to defuse them or what might set them off. We learned to land gently. We stayed calm, made breezy motions, breathed in through our noses and out through our mouths. When the wind blew, we bent with it. When the rivers dragged us downstream, we tried to make ourselves small and soft around the rocks. After many months of pretending we were dead, someone finally thought to cut the danger out. We watched her press her knife to her belly, watched the knife enter the flesh and come back empty and red. Nothing to remove or prove there had ever been a bomb. Nothing that even bled.

RELAXATION TAPE

We were asked to start with our eyes open. The loudspeaker asked us to imagine that we were made of jelly, to let our bodies melt like salt into the mud. We looked skyward and the tape became a prayer. *Let your lips uncouple, your jaws dissolve; let your mouth fall open.* We did. We opened our mouths onto the dark woods. *And now imagine that your bones are leaves.* I saw the melted trees, the acid-rained twigs. *And now imagine your mouth is soil.* I drew night air through the hole in my face. I shut my eyes and imagined them sinking from their sockets and through my skull to leave two open eyes blacking the back of my head. I took what used to be my hand and let it rest on what used to be my stomach. *Imagine you are nothing.* I did not have to imagine. The membranes over my organs had melted. I was already half-mud. *Let go*, the voice said, but without ears I could not hear. I only felt the tremor in what used to be my blood.

THE CARRION FLOWER

We found it in the forest—a small, red-petaled well. Some of us could fit our entire hands inside of it. Some of us could fit our heads. We spread our arms to haul it from the ground. It seemed to weigh the weight of a child, though none of us had seen one in a while. *They looked like us*, someone said, *only small. Like dolls*, said someone else. We all remembered the weight of them on our laps, our knees. We remembered building them houses in the trees, balancing their soft mass above us as we lay on the leaves. But no one could conjure the pitch of their voices or the shape of their cheeks. And no one wanted to let the flower go, so we took turns hefting it up and down the forest's uneven aisles. Some of us bore it better than others. Some of us didn't even gag at the body bag smell. I for one held no perfumed rag to my nose, dreamt of no sweet roses. When the flies arrived I opened my mouth as wide as it would go.

THE KITTENS

The jellyfish was starting to stink. Its fragrant weight unspooled behind us like a loose bobbin. Its pulp bled from the burlap bag as we dragged it across the desert. We couldn't drag it forever. As children we remembered seeing bag after bag of kittens carried away toward the river. I thought of ourselves, long dead without knowing it, only just now realizing we weren't breathing. How was the dust still here? How could we think about the kittens? We were dragging ourselves behind us through the desert. There wasn't enough time. The thought of kittens was 98 percent water and rapidly evaporating. Beneath each grain of sand was an anti-grain. Beneath each memory of kittens was an anti-kitten, an anti-memory, a shadow-shape that darkened the desert. Our mouths were full of hazard. We pulled at the gunnysack with our fingers. Did we also yowl as we were born into the black water?

BOG BODY

Our torsos were swamps we swam in. All the time surrounded by sphagnum. We knew we would become carbon sinks, but just now we had to keep moving, keep our bog bodies afloat. We thought that maybe time would repair us, but here we were paddling with one wrist loose, a kneecap gone missing. Somewhere, space was collecting all these lost things. We imagined it as a bog through which our parts would sink and be held, pickled, in tannic water. That was one of our better thoughts. It helped us live longer. When we found safe places we stopped and buried our faces in the ditches of our hands. Water wept through our finger-reeds, seeped through the sedge. While we slept we ran hedge mazes to try and separate ourselves from our peaty smell. We had terrible dreams where everything we had ever lost was returned to us. Some woke with tears in their ears. Some refused to wake at all. Every day someone would sit down and wait to be eaten by moss. The valley had never been so soft.

REAP

With our heads loose and wobbling, we did strange things. Someone climbed to the top of a tower and flew off. Someone chewed through a pound of shredded cans. I stuck both my hands inside a rattlesnake den and clapped until my arms broke off at the elbow. They thrashed rustedly at my feet, filling the clouds with creaking. In a nearby field I found a body with all its parts intact and dragged it to the factory. I passed someone filling their boots with snow. I passed someone burning a pile of their own hair. On their bare head I could see the bolts, the blue maps drawn in crayon: *dig here* and *don't dig here*. I could see the head tilting on its axis, the hair-smoke scudding around it. At the factory, I attached my new arms as best I could. Everything I held was a little crooked. My face trembled like an unshelled egg. When I reached down to touch the earth it shied away and fled.

RELAXATION TAPE

Some of us didn't have lungs left. So when we lay beneath the loudspeaker sky—when we were told to *pay attention to our breath*—we had to improvise. At the burn pit I'd found a concertina and hooked it to my chest. Now, when told to *inhale to the count of three*, I pulled apart its honeycomb bellows and felt myself fill. I pushed them together and air moved through my mouth like wind through a dead canyon. The bellows inhaled again. I remembered the rhythm of breathing, the ease of it, the mindless fall and rise, the non-travail. *And now exhale*, the static sang. *And now imagine a billowing sail.* I saw the waves behind my eyes, the bobbing boat. *Count back from five.* The ocean swelled. *And now from four.* The ocean burned with oil. *From three.* I opened my eyes. Everyone pumped their squeeze-boxes. The breeze of it flushed vultures from the trees.

We saw them from the top of the hill. The wind blew past our ears and down into the valley where they straggled, up to their tails in snow. One spotted, one striped, one the color of dead leaves. Our encyclopedia had told us about animals, but none of us had ever seen a real one. To see the last of something wasn't new. We had seen many last things: the last acorn, the last lightning storm, the last tide. All the last things had the same smell—a solvent we could taste on the air—which is how we always knew to pay attention. The animals were moving steadily across the valley. We passed around the encyclopedia and studied the pictures, but none of them matched. Someone broke a stick from the last tree and tried to scratch the animals' outlines into the frozen dirt of the last vegetable patch, but it wouldn't take. The animals were crossing the valley faster than we could follow. Our nails broke as we raked at the soil. When we next looked up, our eyes filled with snow.

NIGHT VISION

The earth turned more slowly now. Nights were days long, and days were overcast with coal. So much darkness made our eyes bulge like plums, made them lodestones. We became swift. We became deft hunters. We could see deeply into each other, all the way to the marrow. When one of us stood against the moon, the others watched her blood rush through her like a river. We saw the air bubbles where the stomach and heart should be. And if we didn't blink we could watch them shrink. And if we didn't breathe we could feel our own cells tighten into pebbles. If we wanted, we could scoop handfuls of ourselves into the well we stood at the bottom of and thereby build ourselves a stairway out. Once out, we would face the sky with meteorite eyes. Would see the end of it for the first time.

THE LODESTARS

The grief did not bear down on us. Nor did the panic, nor the despair. Instead they rose through the wells of our bodies like mercury. If we stood still for too long, our heels softened into sponges and we drew grief up into us from the mud or the tarmac. Sometimes we dangled our feet in the ocean to feel the alarm of salt on our skin. Sometimes we woke to find the tide had risen while we slept and terror had collared our necks. We ached for the jellyfish we had drug inland, picturing its nerve net pulsing immortally through that water. Most of us only stood still in shifts, but some planted themselves like signposts, like lodestars. Sometimes we passed their balefire bodies on the highways. The scarecrow eyes that burned a fever in our own. The stiff, spread arms that marked a path of no return. In our watchtowers we stood and narrated their patterns into new myths we had always known. Once upon a time the soil raised a blade to our throats. Once upon a time the sun wiped its bloody hand across us while we slept.

NOTES AND ACKNOWLEDGMENTS

The definitions of "wilder" cited in the epigraph and of "rove" in "Red Rover" are taken from the Oxford English Dictionary.

The italicized lines in "Aftersky" are taken from Amy Clampitt, "The Cove"; John Baillie, *An Essay on the Sublime*; Henry King, "The Exequy"; Jorge Luis Borges, "The Library of Babel"; Alice Fulton, "Slate"; Walt Whitman, "When Lilacs Last in Dooryard Bloom'd"; and Lewis Thomas, *The Lives of a Cell*.

The erasures are all taken from Carl Sagan's *Cosmos* (New York: Random House, 1980). The names in lines 20–21 of "The Meadow, the Lake" are taken from these erased portions.

Grateful acknowledgment is made to the editors of the following journals where these poems, sometimes in earlier versions and under different titles, first appeared:
Anthropoid: "Fuse"
Bennington Review: "Simon Says" and "Descent"
The Collapsar: "Afterbodies," "Breach," and "State of Emergency"
DIAGRAM: "Beginning," "The Jellyfish," and "Misery Rift"
Elsewhere: "Relaxation Tape" ["We listened to relaxation tapes"]
Fairy Tale Review: "D" and "G"
Fog Machine: "No Stars" and "Almanac"
Foundry: "Where I Went Afterward"
Glass: A Journal of Poetry: "The Last Animals"
Handsome: "The Lodestars"
Newfound: "Bog Body" and "The Pit"
PANK: "Relaxation Tape" ["We were asked to start"] and "Relaxation Tape" ["Nightmares were spreading"]
Paperbag: "Reap" and "Night Vision"
Queen Mob's Teahouse: "How I Dreamed There"

Saltfront: "[We Grow Up Frozen]," "[The Ocean Calls]," "[We Had a Taste for Error]," "[An Alien General Collected Us]," and "[The World Is Very Distant]"

TXTOBJX: "Relaxation Tape" ["Some of us didn't have lungs left"] and "The Factory"

What Rough Beast (Indolent Books): "The Witch"

Winter Tangerine: "The Carrion Flower"

The erasures and poems in section three have appeared as the chapbook *Night Vision* (Tucson, AZ: New Michigan Press, 2017).

Galactic thanks to Daniel Lupton and Susannah Nevison for reading drafts on drafts on drafts on drafts.

Thank you to the Loft Literary Center and the Madeline Island School of the Arts for providing me with a fellowship that inspired some of these poems.

Daniel Lupton

CLAIRE WAHMANHOLM is the author of *Night Vision*, winner of the 2017 New Michigan Press/DIAGRAM chapbook competition. Her poems have appeared in *Paperbag, PANK, Saltfront, Waxwing, Bennington Review, The Collapsar, Newfound, New Poetry from the Midwest 2017, 32 Poems, Best New Poets 2015, Memorious, The Journal,* and *Kenyon Review Online.* Her second collection, *Redmouth,* is forthcoming from Tinderbox Editions in 2019. She lives and teaches in the Twin Cities.

The seventh award of

THE LINDQUIST & VENNUM PRIZE FOR POETRY

is presented to

CLAIRE WAHMANHOLM

by

MILKWEED EDITIONS
and
THE LINDQUIST & VENNUM FOUNDATION

Established in 2011, the annual Lindquist & Vennum Prize for Poetry awards $10,000 and publication by Milkweed Editions to a poet residing in North Dakota, South Dakota, Minnesota, Iowa, or Wisconsin. Finalists are selected from among all entrants by the editors of Milkweed Editions. The winning collection is selected annually by an independent judge. The 2018 Lindquist & Vennum Prize for Poetry was judged by Rick Barot.

Milkweed Editions is one of the nation's leading independent publishers, with a mission to identify, nurture, and publish transformative literature, and build an engaged community around it. The Lindquist & Vennum Foundation was established by the Minneapolis-headquartered law firm of Lindquist & Vennum, LLP, and is a donor-advised fund of The Minneapolis Foundation.

milkweed
editions

Founded as a nonprofit organization in 1980,
Milkweed Editions is an independent publisher. Our mission
is to identify, nurture and publish transformative literature,
and build an engaged community around it.

milkweed.org

Adobe Caslon Pro was created by Carol Twombly for Adobe Systems in 1990. Her design was inspired by the family of typefaces cut by the celebrated engraver William Caslon I, whose family foundry served England with clean, elegant type from the early Enlightenment through the turn of the twentieth century.